A Mystery for Mickey Maloney

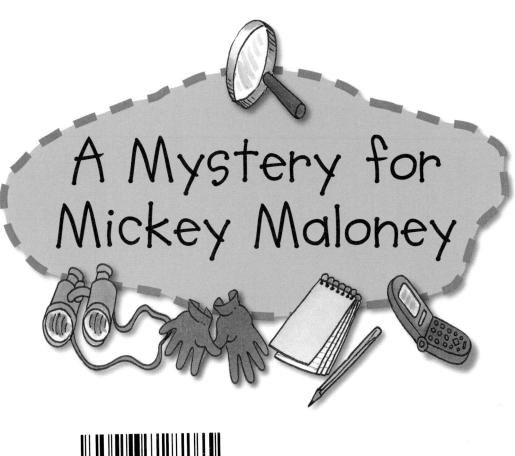

Written by Jill Eggleton

Illustrated by Trevor Pye

One morning, when Mickey Maloney woke up, he saw a pile of rubbish in his garden.

"How did all that rubbish get there?" he said.

Mickey Maloney was a spy – a very tidy spy. He didn't like rubbish anywhere. He picked it up and put it in the bin.

The next morning,
there was another pile
of rubbish in the garden!
Mickey Maloney took it away.

4

That night,
Mickey Maloney climbed
up a tree with his spy
glasses.

"Someone is dumping
their rubbish here,"
he said. "No one can
dump rubbish in my garden.
I, Mickey Maloney,
will catch them."

Mickey Maloney waited and waited and waited. Then he saw a dog . . . a little white dog, with hair like a mop. She came wriggling under the fence. In her mouth she had some rubbish!

"A dog!" said Mickey Maloney.
He got down from the tree.
"**Stop!**" he shouted.

The dog saw Mickey Maloney.
She dropped the rubbish
and ran back to the fence.

But she was going so fast she
couldn't stop. She crashed into
the fence with a big **THUD!**

Mickey Maloney picked her up. "You're hurt," he said. "I'll have to take you inside."

"You're better now," he said.
"You can go home."
And he put the dog out the gate.

"Go home!" he said.
"And don't bring rubbish
to my house again."

But the dog wouldn't go.
She barked at the gate
until Mickey Maloney let her in.

"Don't you have a home?"
said Mickey Maloney.

She barked louder and louder.
"I will have to find your home then,"
he said.

So Mickey Maloney put
an advertisement in the paper.
He waited for weeks and weeks,
but no one came for the dog.

Found
Small white dog
with hair like
a mop.
Likes rubbish!
Phone
MM 07638281

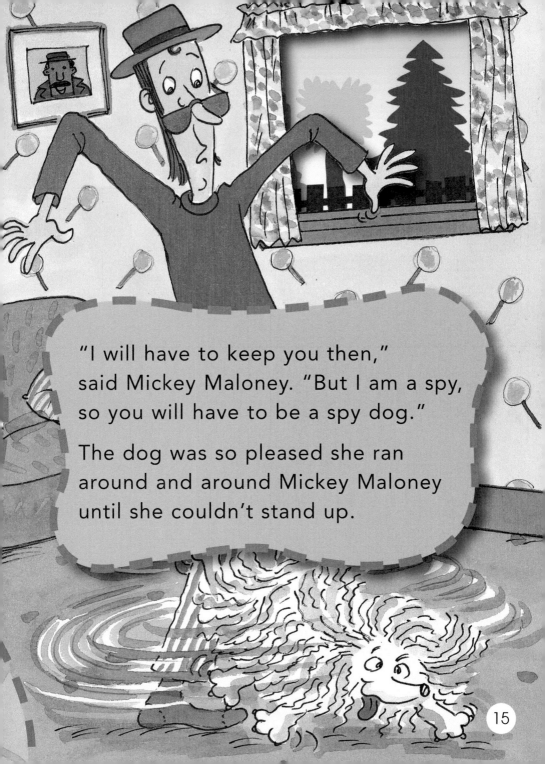

"I will have to keep you then," said Mickey Maloney. "But I am a spy, so you will have to be a spy dog."

The dog was so pleased she ran around and around Mickey Maloney until she couldn't stand up.

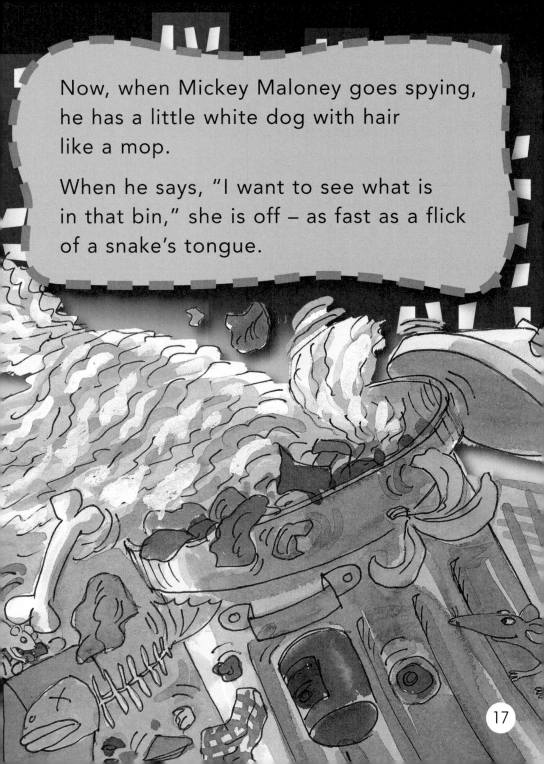

Now, when Mickey Maloney goes spying, he has a little white dog with hair like a mop.

When he says, "I want to see what is in that bin," she is off – as fast as a flick of a snake's tongue.

Advertisements

Advertisements can look different.

Newspaper advertisement

—FOUND—
Hairy, white dog.
Likes rubbish.
Very friendly.
Is this your dog?
Phone Mickey Maloney
Tel: 07638281

Flyer advertisement

Guide Notes

Title: A Mystery for Mickey Maloney
Stage: Launching Fluency – Orange

Genre: Fiction
Approach: Guided Reading
Processes: Thinking Critically, Exploring Language, Processing Information
Written and Visual Focus: Advertisements, Speech Bubbles
Word Count: 386

THINKING CRITICALLY
(sample questions)
- What do you think this story could be about? Look at the title and discuss.
- Look at the cover. What do you think Mickey Maloney could be doing?
- Look at pages 2 and 3. Where do you think the rubbish could have come from?
- Look at pages 4 and 5. Mickey Maloney thought it was a person dumping rubbish. Why do you think he thought that?
- Look at pages 6 and 7. Why do you think the dog was taking the rubbish into Mickey Maloney's garden?
- Look at pages 10 and 11. What do you think made Mickey Maloney think the dog was better?
- Look at pages 14 and 15. Why do you think no one came for the dog?
- Look at pages 16 and 17. What do you think is meant by *as fast as a flick of a snake's tongue*?

EXPLORING LANGUAGE

Terminology
Author and illustrator credits, ISBN number

Vocabulary
Clarify: pile, dump, advertisement, mop
Singular/Plural: week/weeks
Homonyms: week/weak, saw/sore

Print Conventions
Apostrophes – possessive (snake's tongue), contractions (didn't, you're, I'll, couldn't, don't); dash

Print Conventions
Focus on short and long vowels **i** (p**i**le, rubb**i**sh, n**i**ght, d**i**d, t**i**dy, b**i**n)
Discuss suffix and base words (dropp**ed**, climb**ed**)